The Years Between

By Rudyard Kipling

GARDEN CITY   NEW YORK
DOUBLEDAY, PAGE & COMPANY
1919

TO THE SEVEN WATCHMEN

Seven watchmen sitting in a tower,
   Watching what had come upon mankind,
Showed the Man the Glory and the Power,
   And bade him shape the Kingdom to his mind.
'All things on Earth your will shall win you.'
   ('Twas so their counsel ran)
'But the Kingdom—the Kingdom is within you,'
   Said the Man's own mind to the Man.
        For time, and some time—
As it was in the bitter years before
   So it shall be in the over-sweetened hour—
That a man's mind is wont to tell him more
   Than Seven Watchmen sitting in a tower.

CONTENTS

CONTENTS

INDEX TO FIRST LINES

xi

INDEX TO FIRST LINES

THE YEARS BETWEEN

THE ROWERS

1902

(When Germany proposed that England should help her in a
naval demonstration to collect debts from Venezuela.)

THE banked oars fell an hundred strong,
   And backed and threshed and ground,
But bitter was the rowers' song
   As they brought the war-boat round.

They had no heart for the rally and roar
   That makes the whale-bath smoke—
When the great blades cleave and hold and leave
   As one on the racing stroke.

They sang:—'What reckoning do you keep,
   And steer by her what star,
If we come unscathed from the Southern deep
   To be wrecked on a Baltic bar?

3

'Last night you swore our voyage was done,
  But seaward still we go.
And you tell us now of a secret vow
  You have made with an open foe!

'That we must lie off a lightless coast
  And haul and back and veer,
At the will of the breed that have wronged us most
  For a year and a year and a year!

'There was never a shame in Christendie
  They laid not to our door—
And you say we must take the winter sea
  And sail with them once more?

'Look South! The gale is scarce o'erpast
  That stripped and laid us down,
When we stood forth but they stood fast
  And prayed to see us drown.

'Our dead they mocked are scarcely cold,
　Our wounds are bleeding yet—
And you tell us now that our strength is sold
　To help them press for a debt!

' 'Neath all the flags of all mankind
　That use upon the seas,
Was there no other fleet to find
　That you strike hands with these?

'Of evil times that men can choose
　On evil fate to fall,
What brooding Judgment let you loose
　To pick the worst of all?

'In sight of peace—from the Narrow Seas
　O'er half the world to run—
With a cheated crew, to league anew
　With the Goth and the shameless Hun!'

THE VETERANS

(Written for the gathering of survivors of the Indian Mutiny,
Albert Hall, 1907.)

To-day, across our fathers' graves,
  The astonished years reveal
The remnant of that desperate host
  Which cleansed our East with steel.

Hail and farewell! We greet you here,
  With tears that none will scorn—
O Keepers of the House of old,
  Or ever we were born!

One service more we dare to ask—
  Pray for us, heroes, pray,
That when Fate lays on us our task
  We do not shame the Day!

THE DECLARATION OF LONDON

JUNE 29, 1911

('On the re-assembling of Parliament after the Coronation, the
Government have no intention of allowing their followers
to vote according to their convictions on the Declaration
of London, but insist on a strictly party vote.'—*Daily
Papers.*)

WE were all one heart and one race
   When the Abbey trumpets blew.
For a moment's breathing-space
   We had forgotten you.
Now you return to your honoured place
   Panting to shame us anew.

We have walked with the Ages dead—
   With our Past alive and ablaze.
And you bid us pawn our honour for bread,
   This day of all the days!

And you cannot wait till our guests are sped,
  Or last week's wreath decays?

The light is still in our eyes
  Of Faith and Gentlehood,
Of Service and Sacrifice;
  And it does not match our mood,
To turn so soon to your treacheries
  That starve our land of her food.

Our ears still carry the sound
  Of our once Imperial seas,
Exultant after our King was crowned,
  Beneath the sun and the breeze.
It is too early to have them bound
  Or sold at your decrees.

Wait till the memory goes,
  Wait till the visions fade,
We may betray in time, God knows,
  But we would not have it said,
When you make report to our scornful foes,
  That we kissed as we betrayed!

ULSTER

1912

('Their webs shall not become garments, neither shall they
cover themselves with their works: their works are works
of iniquity and the act of violence is in their hands.'—
Isaiah lix. 6.)

THE dark eleventh hour
Draws on and sees us sold
To every evil power
We fought against of old.
Rebellion, rapine, hate,
Oppression, wrong and greed
Are loosed to rule our fate,
By England's act and deed.

The Faith in which we stand,
The laws we made and guard,

Our honour, lives, and land
Are given for reward
To Murder done by night,
To Treason taught by day,
To folly, sloth, and spite,
And we are thrust away.

The blood our fathers spilt,
Our love, our toils, our pains,
Are counted us for guilt,
And only bind our chains.
Before an Empire's eyes
The traitor claims his price.
What need of further lies?
We are the sacrifice.

We asked no more than leave
To reap where we had sown,
Through good and ill to cleave
To our own flag and throne.

Now England's shot and steel
Beneath that flag must show
How loyal hearts should kneel
To England's oldest foe.

We know the war prepared
On every peaceful home,
We know the hells declared
For such as serve not Rome—
The terror, threats, and dread
In market, hearth, and field—
We know, when all is said,
We perish if we yield.

Believe, we dare not boast,
Believe, we do not fear—
We stand to pay the cost
In all that men hold dear.
What answer from the North?
One Law, one Land, one Throne.
If England drive us forth
We shall not fall alone.

THE COVENANT

1914

WE thought we ranked above the chance of ill.
  Others might fall, not we, for we were wise—
Merchants in freedom.   So, of our free-will
  We let our servants drug our strength with lies.
The pleasure and the poison had its way
  On us as on the meanest, till we learned
That he who lies will steal, who steals will slay.
  Neither God's judgment nor man's heart was
    turned.

Yet there remains His Mercy—to be sought
Through wrath and peril till we cleanse the wrong
By that last right which our forefathers claimed

When their Law failed them and its stewards were
    bought.
This is our cause.   God help us, and make strong
Our wills to meet Him later, unashamed!

FRANCE

1913

Broke to every known mischance, lifted over all
By the light sane joy of life, the buckler of the Gaul;
Furious in luxury, merciless in toil,
Terrible with strength that draws from her tireless soil;
Strictest judge of her own worth, gentlest of man's
*   mind,*
First to follow Truth and last to leave old Truths
*   behind—*
France, beloved of every soul that loves its fellow-kind !

Ere our birth (rememberest thou?) side by side we
    lay
Fretting in the womb of Rome to begin our fray.

14

Ere men knew our tongues apart, our one task was
    known—

Each must mould the other's fate as he wrought
    his own.

To this end we stirred mankind till all Earth was
    ours,

Till our world-end strifes begat wayside thrones
    and powers—

Puppets that we made or broke to bar the other's
    path—

Necessary, outpost folk, hirelings of our wrath.

To this end we stormed the seas, tack for tack, and
    burst

Through the doorways of new worlds, doubtful
    which was first,

Hand on hilt (rememberest thou?) ready for the
    blow—

Sure, whatever else we met, we should meet our foe.

Spurred or baulked at every stride by the other's
    strength,

So we rode the ages down and every ocean's length!

Where did you refrain from us or we refrain from
   you?
Ask the wave that has not watched war between
   us two!
Others held us for a while, but with weaker charms,
These we quitted at the call for each other's
   arms.
Eager toward the known delight, equally we strove—
Each the other's mystery, terror, need, and love.
To each other's open court with our proofs we
   came.
Where could we find honour else, or men to test
   our claim?
From each other's throat we wrenched—valour's
   last reward—
That extorted word of praise gasped 'twixt lunge
   and guard.
In each other's cup we poured mingled blood and
   tears,
Brutal joys, unmeasured hopes, intolerable fears—
All that soiled or salted life for a thousand years.

Proved beyond the need of proof, matched in every
    clime,
O companion, we have lived greatly through all
    time!

Yoked in knowledge and remorse, now we come to
    rest,
Laughing at old villainies that Time has turned to
    jest;
Pardoning old necessities no pardon can efface—
That undying sin we shared in Rouen market-place.
Now we watch the new years shape, wondering if
    they hold
Fiercer lightnings in their heart than we launched
    of old.
Now we hear new voices rise, question, boast or gird,
As we raged (rememberest thou?) when our crowds
    were stirred.
Now we count new keels afloat, and new hosts on
    land,

Massed like ours (rememberest thou?) when our
strokes were planned.

We were schooled for dear life's sake, to know each
other's blade.

What can blood and iron make more than we have
made?

We have learned by keenest use to know each
other's mind.

What shall blood and iron loose that we cannot
bind?

We who swept each other's coast, sacked each
other's home,

Since the sword of Brennus clashed on the scales
at Rome

Listen, count and close again, wheeling girth to
girth,

In the linked and steadfast guard set for peace on
earth!

Broke to every known mischance, lifted over all

By the light sane joy of life, the buckler of the Gaul;

Furious in luxury, merciless in toil,

Terrible with strength renewed from a tireless soil;

Strictest judge of her own worth, gentlest of man's
mind,

First to face the Truth and last to leave old Truths
behind—

France, beloved of every soul that loves or serves its
kind!

'FOR ALL WE HAVE AND ARE'

1914

For all we have and are,
For all our children's fate,
Stand up and take the war,
The Hun is at the gate!
Our world has passed away,
In wantonness o'erthrown.
There is nothing left to-day
But steel and fire and stone!

Though all we knew depart,
The old Commandments stand:—
'In courage keep your heart,
In strength lift up your hand.'

Once more we hear the word
That sickened earth of old:—
'No law except the Sword
Unsheathed and uncontrolled.'
Once more it knits mankind,
Once more the nations go
To meet and break and bind
A crazed and driven foe.

Comfort, content, delight,
The ages' slow-bought gain,
They shrivelled in a night.
Only ourselves remain
To face the naked days
In silent fortitude,
Through perils and dismays
Renewed and re-renewed.
    Though all we made depart,
    The old Commandments stand:—
    'In patience keep your heart,
    In strength lift up your hand.'

No easy hope or lies
Shall bring us to our goal,
But iron sacrifice
Of body, will, and soul.
There is but one task for all—
One life for each to give.
Who stands if Freedom fall?
Who dies if England live?

A SONG IN STORM

BE well assured that on our side
  The abiding oceans fight,
Though headlong wind and heaping tide
  Make us their sport to-night.
By force of weather not of war
  In jeopardy we steer,
Then welcome Fate's discourtesy
  Whereby it shall appear,
    How in all time of our distress,
    And our deliverance too,
    The game is more than the player of the game,
    And the ship is more than the crew.

Out of the mist into the mirk
  The glimmering combers roll.
Almost these mindless waters work
  As though they had a soul—

Almost as though they leagued to whelm
　　Our flag beneath their green:
Then welcome Fate's discourtesy
　　Whereby it shall be seen, etc.

Be well assured, though wave and wind
　　Have weightier blows in store,
That we who keep the watch assigned
　　Must stand to it the more;
And as our streaming bows rebuke
　　Each billow's baulked career,
Sing, welcome Fate's discourtesy
　　Whereby it is made clear, etc.

No matter though our deck be swept
　　And masts and timber crack—
We can make good all loss except
　　The loss of turning back.
So, 'twixt these Devils and our deep
　　Let courteous trumpets sound,
To welcome Fate's discourtesy
　　Whereby it will be found, etc.

Be well assured, though in our power
  Is nothing left to give
But chance and place to meet the hour,
  And leave to strive to live,
Till these dissolve our Order holds,
  Our Service binds us here.
Then welcome Fate's discourtesy
  Whereby it is made clear,
    How in all time of our distress,
    And in our triumph too,
    The game is more than the player of the game,
    And the ship is more than the crew!

THE OUTLAWS

1914

THROUGH learned and laborious years
　They set themselves to find
Fresh terrors and undreamed-of fears
　To heap upon mankind.

All that they drew from Heaven above
　Or digged from earth beneath,
They laid into their treasure-trove
　And arsenals of death:

While, for well-weighed advantage sake,
　Ruler and ruled alike
Built up the faith they meant to break
　When the fit hour should strike.

They traded with the careless earth,
    And good return it gave;
They plotted by their neighbour's hearth
    The means to make him slave.

When all was ready to their hand
    They loosed their hidden sword,
And utterly laid waste a land
    Their oath was pledged to guard.

Coldly they went about to raise
    To life and make more dread
Abominations of old days,
    That men believed were dead.

They paid the price to reach their goal
    Across a world in flame;
But their own hate slew their own soul
    Before that victory came.

ZION

The Doorkeepers of Zion,
  They do not always stand
In helmet and whole armour,
  With halberds in their hand;
But, being sure of Zion,
  And all her mysteries,
They rest awhile in Zion,
Sit down and smile in Zion;
Ay, even jest in Zion;
  In Zion, at their ease.

The Gatekeepers of Baal,
  They dare not sit or lean,
But fume and fret and posture
  And foam and curse between;

For being bound to Baal,
  Whose sacrifice is vain,
Their rest is scant with Baal,
They glare and pant for Baal,
They mouth and rant for Baal,
  For Baal in their pain!

But we will go to Zion,
  By choice and not through dread,
With these our present comrades
  And those our present dead;
And, being free of Zion
  In both her fellowships,
Sit down and sup in Zion—
Stand up and drink in Zion
Whatever cup in Zion
  Is offered to our lips!

LORD ROBERTS

1914

He passed in the very battle-smoke
  Of the war that he had descried.
Three hundred mile of cannon spoke
  When the Master-Gunner died.

He passed to the very sound of the guns;
  But, before his eye grew dim,
He had seen the faces of the sons
  Whose sires had served with him.

He had touched their sword-hilts and greeted each
  With the old sure word of praise;
And there was virtue in touch and speech
  As it had been in old days.

So he dismissed them and took his rest,
   And the steadfast spirit went forth
Between the adoring East and West
   And the tireless guns of the North.

Clean, simple, valiant, well-beloved,
   Flawless in faith and fame,
Whom neither ease nor honours moved
   An hair's-breadth from his aim.

Never again the war-wise face,
   The weighed and urgent word
That pleaded in the market-place—
   Pleaded and was not heard!

Yet from his life a new life springs
   Through all the hosts to come,
And Glory is the least of things
   That follow this man home.

THE QUESTION

1916

Brethren, how shall it fare with me
  When the war is laid aside,
If it be proven that I am he
  For whom a world has died?

If it be proven that all my good,
  And the greater good I will make,
Were purchased me by a multitude
  Who suffered for my sake?

That I was delivered by mere mankind
  Vowed to one sacrifice,
And not, as I hold them, battle-blind,
  But dying with open eyes?

That they did not ask me to draw the sword
  When they stood to endure their lot—
That they only looked to me for a word,
  And I answered I knew them not?

If it be found, when the battle clears,
  Their death has set me free,
Then how shall I live with myself through the
    years
  Which they have bought for me?

Brethren, how must it fare with me,
  Or how am I justified,
If it be proven that I am he
  For whom mankind has died
If it be proven that I am he
  Who being questioned denied?

THE CHOICE

1917

(THE AMERICAN SPIRIT SPEAKS)

To the Judge of Right and Wrong
With Whom fulfilment lies
Our purpose and our power belong,
Our faith and sacrifice.

Let Freedom's Land rejoice!
Our ancient bonds are riven;
Once more to us the eternal choice
Of Good or Ill is given.

Not at a little cost,
Hardly by prayer or tears,
Shall we recover the road we lost
In the drugged and doubting years.

But, after the fires and the wrath,
  But, after searching and pain,
His Mercy opens us a path
  To live with ourselves again.

In the Gates of Death rejoice!
  We see and hold the good—
Bear witness, Earth, we have made our choice
  With Freedom's brotherhood!

Then praise the Lord Most High
  Whose Strength hath saved us whole,
Who bade us choose that the Flesh should die
  And not the living Soul!

  To the God in Man displayed—
    Where e'er we see that Birth,
  Be love and understanding paid
    As never yet on earth!

To the Spirit that moves in Man,
On Whom all worlds depend,
Be Glory since our world began
And service to the end!

THE HOLY WAR

1917

('For here lay the excellent wisdom of him that built Mansoul,
that the walls could never be broken down nor hurt by the
most mighty adverse potentate unless the townsmen gave
consent thereto.'—BUNYAN'S *Holy War*.)

A TINKER out of Bedford,
  A vagrant oft in quod,
A private under Fairfax,
  A minister of God—
Two hundred years and thirty
  Ere Armageddon came
His single hand portrayed it,
  And Bunyan was his name!

He mapped, for those who follow,
  The world in which we are—
'This famous town of Mansoul'
  That takes the Holy War.

Her true and traitor people,
   The gates along her wall,
From Eye Gate unto Feel Gate,
   John Bunyan showed them all.

All enemy divisions,
   Recruits of every class,
And highly-screened positions
   For flame or poison-gas;
The craft that we call modern,
   The crimes that we call new,
John Bunyan had 'em typed and filed
   In Sixteen Eighty-two.

Likewise the Lords of Looseness
   That hamper faith and works,
The Perseverance-Doubters,
   And Present-Comfort shirks,
With brittle intellectuals
   Who crack beneath a strain—
John Bunyan met that helpful set
   In Charles the Second's reign.

Emmanuel's vanguard dying
  For right and not for rights,
My Lord Apollyon lying
  To the State-kept Stockholmites,
The Pope, the swithering Neutrals,
  The Kaiser and his Gott—
Their rôles, their goals, their naked
    souls—
  He knew and drew the lot.

Now he hath left his quarters
  In Bunhill Fields to lie,
The wisdom that he taught us
  Is proven prophecy—
One watchword through our armies,
  One answer from our lands:—
'No dealings with Diabolus
  As long as Mansoul stands!'

A pedlar from a hovel,
  The lowest of the low,

The father of the Novel,
Salvation's first Defoe,
Eight blinded generations
Ere Armageddon came,
He showed us how to meet it,
And Bunyan was his name!

THE HOUSES

(A SONG OF THE DOMINIONS)

1898

'TWIXT my house and thy house the pathway is
  broad,
In thy house or my house is half the world's hoard;
By my house and thy house hangs all the world's
  fate,
On thy house and my house lies half the world's
  hate.

For my house and thy house no help shall we find
Save thy house and my house—kin cleaving to
  kind:
If my house be taken, thine tumbleth anon,
If thy house be forfeit, mine followeth soon.

41

'Twixt my house and thy house what talk can
    there be
Of headship or lordship, or service or fee?
Since my house to thy house no greater can send
Than thy house to my house—friend comforting
    friend;
And thy house to my house no meaner can bring
Than my house to thy house—King counselling
    King.

RUSSIA TO THE PACIFISTS

God rest you, peaceful gentlemen, let nothing you
 dismay,
But—leave your sports a little while—the dead are
 borne this way!
Armies dead and Cities dead, past all count or care.
God rest you, merry gentlemen, what portent see
 you there?
  Singing:—Break ground for a wearied host
   That have no ground to keep.
   Give them the rest that they covet
   most . . .
   And who shall next to sleep, good sirs,
   In such a trench to sleep?

God rest you, peaceful gentlemen, but give us
 leave to pass.
We go to dig a nation's grave as great as England
 was.

For this Kingdom and this Glory and this Power
    and this Pride

Three hundred years it flourished—in three hundred
    days it died.

      Singing:—Pour oil for a frozen throng,
          That lie about the ways.
          Give them the warmth they have lacked
            so long . . .
          And what shall be next to blaze, good
            sirs,
          On such a pyre to blaze?

God rest you, thoughtful gentlemen, and send your
    sleep is light!

Remains of this dominion no shadow, sound, or sight,

Except the sound of weeping and the sight of burn-
    ing fire,

And the shadow of a people that is trampled into
    mire.

      Singing:—Break bread for a starving folk
          That perish in the field.

Give them their food as they take the
  yoke . . .
And who shall be next to yield, good
  sirs,
For such a bribe to yield?

God rest you, merry gentlemen, and keep you in
  your mirth!
Was ever kingdom turned so soon to ashes, blood,
  and earth?
'Twixt the summer and the snow—seeding-time and
  frost—
Arms and victual, hope and counsel, name and
  country lost!
     Singing:—*Let down by the foot and the head—*
          Shovel and smooth it all !
          So do we bury a Nation dead . . .
          And who shall be next to fall, good
            sirs,
          With your good help to fall?

THE IRISH GUARDS

1918

WE'RE not so old in the Army List,
    But we're not so young at our trade,
For we had the honour at Fontenoy
    Of meeting the Guards' Brigade.
'Twas Lally, Dillon, Bulkeley, Clare,
    And Lee that led us then,
And after a hundred and seventy years
    We're fighting for France again!
        Old Days ! The wild geese are flighting,
            Head to the storm as they faced it before !
        For where there are Irish there's bound to be
            fighting,
        And when there's no fighting, it's Ireland no more !
                                Ireland no more !

The fashion's all for khaki now,
  But once through France we went
Full-dressed in scarlet Army cloth,
  The English—left at Ghent.
They're fighting on our side to-day
  But, before they changed their clothes,
The half of Europe knew our fame,
  As all of Ireland knows!

Old Days !   The wild geese are flying,
    Head to the storm as they faced it before !
  For where there are Irish there's memory undying,
    And when we forget, it is Ireland no more !
                              Ireland no more !

From Barry Wood to Gouzeaucourt,
  From Boyne to Pilkem Ridge,
The ancient days come back no more
  Than water under the bridge.

But the bridge it stands and the water runs
 As red as yesterday,
And the Irish move to the sound of the guns
 Like salmon to the sea.

  Old Days ! The wild geese are ranging,
   Head to the storm as they faced it before !
  For where there are Irish their hearts are un-
   changing,
   And when they are changed, it is Ireland no
   more !

        Ireland no more !

We're not so old in the Army List,
 But we're not so new in the ring,
For we carried our packs with Marshal Saxe
 When Louis was our King.
But Douglas Haig's our Marshal now
 And we're King George's men,
And after one hundred and seventy years
 We're fighting for France again!

Ah, France !   And did we stand by you,

  When life was made splendid with gifts and
     rewards ?

Ah, France !   And will we deny you

  In the hour of your agony, Mother of Swords ?

Old Days !   The wild geese are flighting,

  Head to the storm as they faced it before !

For where there are Irish there's loving and
     fighting,

And when we stop either, it's Ireland no more !

                              Ireland no more !

A NATIVITY

1916

THE Babe was laid in the Manger
  Between the gentle kine—
All safe from cold and danger—
  'But it was not so with mine.

          (With mine!   With mine!)
'Is it well with the child, is it well?'
  The waiting mother prayed.
'For I know not how he fell,
  And I know not where he is laid.'

A Star stood forth in Heaven;
  The watchers ran to see
The Sign of the Promise given—
  'But there comes no sign to me.

          (To me!   To me!)

'*My* child died in the dark.
   Is it well with the child, is it well?
There was none to tend him or mark,
   And I know not how he fell.'

The Cross was raised on high;
   The Mother grieved beside—
'But the Mother saw Him die
   And took Him when He died.
               (He died!   He died!)
'Seemly and undefiled
   His burial-place was made—
Is it well, is it well with the child?
   For I know not where he is laid.'

On the dawning of Easter Day
   Comes Mary Magdalene;
But the Stone was rolled away,
   And the Body was not within—
               (Within!   Within!)

'Ah, who will answer my word?'
    The broken mother prayed.
'They have taken away my Lord,
    And I know not where He is laid.'

        .   .   .   .

'The Star stands forth in Heaven.
    The watchers watch in vain
For a Sign of the Promise given
    Of peace on Earth again—
                        (Again!   Again!)

'But I know for Whom he fell'—
    The steadfast mother smiled,
'Is it well with the child—is it well?
    It is well—it is well with the child!'

EN–DOR

('Behold there is a woman that hath a familiar spirit at En-dor.'—1 *Samuel* xxviii. 7.)

THE road to En-dor is easy to tread
    For Mother or yearning Wife,
There, it is sure, we shall meet our Dead
    As they were even in life.
Earth has not dreamed of the blessing in store
For desolate hearts on the road to En-dor.

Whispers shall comfort us out of the dark—
    Hands—ah God!—that we knew!
Visions and voices—look and heark!—
    Shall prove that our tale is true,
And that those who have passed to the further
    shore
May be hailed—at a price—on the road to En-dor.

But they are so deep in their new eclipse
  Nothing they say can reach,
Unless it be uttered by alien lips
  And framed in a stranger's speech.
The son must send word to the mother that bore,
Through an hireling's mouth. 'Tis the rule of
    En-dor.

And not for nothing these gifts are shown
  By such as delight our dead.
They must twitch and stiffen and slaver and groan
  Ere the eyes are set in the head,
And the voice from the belly begins.   Therefore,
We pay them a wage where they ply at En-dor.

Even so, we have need of faith
  And patience to follow the clue.
Often, at first, what the dear one saith
  Is babble, or jest, or untrue.

(Lying spirits perplex us sore
Till our loves—and our lives—are well-known at
    En-dor). . . .

Oh the road to En-dor is the oldest road
   And the craziest road of all !
Straight it runs to the Witch's abode,
   As it did in the days of Saul,
And nothing has changed of the sorrow in store
For such as go down on the road to En-dor !

A RECANTATION

(TO LYDE OF THE MUSIC HALLS)

WHAT boots it on the Gods to call?
  Since, answered or unheard,
We perish with the Gods and all
  Things made—except the Word.

Ere certain Fate had touched a heart
  By fifty years made cold,
I judged thee, Lyde, and thy art
  O'erblown and over-bold.

But he—but he, of whom bereft
  I suffer vacant days—
He on his shield not meanly left—
  He cherished all thy lays.

Witness the magic coffer stocked
  With convoluted runes
Wherein thy very voice was locked
  And linked to circling tunes.

Witness thy portrait, smoke-defiled,
  That decked his shelter-place.
Life seemed more present, wrote the child,
  Beneath thy well-known face.

And when the grudging days restored
  Him for a breath to home,
He, with fresh crowds of youth, adored
  Thee making mirth in Rome.

Therefore, I, humble, join the hosts,
  Loyal and loud, who bow
To thee as Queen of Songs—and ghosts—
  For I remember how

Never more rampant rose the Hall
  At thy audacious line
Than when the news came in from Gaul
  Thy son had—followed mine.

But thou didst hide it in thy breast
  And, capering, took the brunt
Of blaze and blare, and launched the jest
  That swept next week the front.

Singer to children!   Ours possessed
  Sleep before noon—but thee,
Wakeful each midnight for the rest,
  No holocaust shall free.

Yet they who use the Word assigned,
  To hearten and make whole,
Not less than Gods have served mankind,
  Though vultures rend their soul.

MY BOY JACK

'HAVE you news of my boy Jack?'
  Not this tide.
'When d'you think that he'll come back?'
  Not with this wind blowing, and this tide.

'Has any one else had word of him?'
  Not this tide.
For what is sunk will hardly swim,
  Not with this wind blowing, and this tide.

'Oh, dear, what comfort can I find?'
  None this tide,
  Nor any tide,
Except he did not shame his kind—
  Not even with that wind blowing, and that tide.

Then hold your head up all the more,
This tide,
And every tide;
Because he was the son you bore,
And gave to that wind blowing and that tide!

THE VERDICTS

(JUTLAND)

NOT in the thick of the fight,
  Not in the press of the odds,
Do the heroes come to their height,
  Or we know the demi-gods.

That stands over till peace.
  We can only perceive
Men returned from the seas,
  Very grateful for leave.

They grant us sudden days
  Snatched from their business of war;
But we are too close to appraise
  What manner of men they are.

And, whether their names go down
　　With age-kept victories,
Or whether they battle and drown
　　Unreckoned, is hid from our eyes.

They are too near to be great,
　　But our children shall understand
When and how our fate
　　Was changed, and by whose hand.

Our children shall measure their worth.
　　We are content to be blind　.　.　.
But we know that we walk on a new-born earth
　　With the saviours of mankind.

MESOPOTAMIA

1917

They shall not return to us, the resolute, the young,
  The eager and whole-hearted whom we gave:
But the men who left them thriftily to die in their
    own dung,
  Shall they come with years and honour to the
    grave?

They shall not return to us, the strong men coldly
    slain
  In sight of help denied from day to day:
But the men who edged their agonies and chid
    them in their pain,
  Are they too strong and wise to put away?

Our dead shall not return to us while Day and
    Night divide—
  Never while the bars of sunset hold:
But the idle-minded overlings who quibbled while
    they died,
  Shall they thrust for high employments as of old?

Shall we only threaten and be angry for an hour?
  When the storm is ended shall we find
How softly but how swiftly they have sidled back
    to power
  By the favour and contrivance of their kind?

Even while they soothe us, while they promise
    large amends,
  Even while they make a show of fear,
Do they call upon their debtors, and take council
    with their friends,
  To confirm and re-establish each career?

Their lives cannot repay us—their death could not
    undo—
  The shame that they have laid upon our race:
But the slothfulness that wasted and the arrogance
    that slew,
  Shall we leave it unabated in its place?

THE HYÆNAS

After the burial-parties leave
  And the baffled kites have fled;
The wise hyænas come out at eve
  To take account of our dead.

How he died and why he died
  Troubles them not a whit.
They snout the bushes and stones aside
  And dig till they come to it.

They are only resolute they shall eat
  That they and their mates may thrive,
And they know that the dead are safer meat
  Than the weakest thing alive.

(For a goat may butt, and a worm may sting,
 And a child will sometimes stand;
But a poor dead soldier of the King
 Can never lift a hand.)

They whoop and halloo and scatter the dirt
 Until their tushes white
Take good hold in the army shirt,
 And tug the corpse to light.

And the pitiful face is shewn again
 For an instant ere they close;
But it is not discovered to living men—
 Only to God and to those

Who, being soulless, are free from shame,
 Whatever meat they may find.
Nor do they defile the dead man's name—
 That is reserved for his kind.

THE SPIES' MARCH

(BEFORE THE WAR)

('The outbreak is in full swing and our death-rate would sicken
Napoleon. . . . Dr. M——died last week, and C——
on Monday, but some more medicines are coming. . .
We don't seem to be able to check it at all. . . . Vil-
lages panicking badly. . . . In some places not a
living soul. . . . But at any rate the experience
gained may come in useful, so I am keeping my notes
written up to date in case of accidents. . . . Death
is a queer chap to live with for steady company.'—*Extract
from a private letter from Manchuria.*)

THERE are no leaders to lead us to honour, and yet
without leaders we sally,
Each man reporting for duty alone, out of sight,
out of reach, of his fellow.
There are no bugles to call the battalions, and yet
without bugles we rally

From the ends of the earth to the ends of the
earth, to follow the Standard of Yellow!
    Fall in! O fall in! O fall in!

Not where the squadrons mass,
    Not where the bayonets shine,
Not where the big shell shout as they pass
    Over the firing-line;
Not where the wounded are,
    Not where the nations die,
Killed in the cleanly game of war—
    That is no place for a spy!
O Princes, Thrones and Powers, your work is
    less than ours—
Here is no place for a spy!

Trained to another use,
    We march with colours furled,
Only concerned when Death breaks loose
    On a front of half a world.

Only for General Death
    The Yellow Flag may fly,
While we take post beneath—
    That is the place for a spy.
Where Plague has spread his pinions over Na-
    tions and Dominions—
Then will be work for a spy!

The dropping shots begin,
    The single funerals pass,
Our skirmishers run in,
    The corpses dot the grass!
The howling towns stampede,
    The tainted hamlets die.
Now it is war indeed—
    Now there is room for a spy!
O Peoples, Kings and Lands, we are waiting
    your commands—
What is the work for a spy?
    (DRUMS)—*Fear is upon us, spy!*

'Go where his pickets hide—
   Unmask the shapes they take,
Whether a gnat from the waterside,
   Or stinging fly in the brake,
Or filth of the crowded street,
   Or a sick rat limping by,
Or a smear of spittle dried in the heat—
   That is the work of a spy!
      (DRUMS)—*Death is upon us, spy!*

'What does he next prepare?
   Whence will he move to attack?—
By water, earth or air?—
   How can we head him back?
Shall we starve him out if we burn
   Or bury his food-supply?
Slip through his lines and learn—
   That is work for a spy!
      (DRUMS)—*Get to your business, spy!*

'Does he feint or strike in force?
  Will he charge or ambuscade?
What is it checks his course?
  Is he beaten or only delayed?
How long will the lull endure?
  Is he retreating?   Why?
Crawl to his camp and make sure—
  That is the work for a spy!
        (DRUMS)—*Fetch us our answer, spy!*

'Ride with him girth to girth
  Wherever the Pale Horse wheels,
Wait on his councils, ear to earth,
  And say what the dust reveals.
For the smoke of our torment rolls
  Where the burning thousands lie;
What do we care for men's bodies or souls?
  Bring us deliverance, spy!'

THE SONS OF MARTHA

The Sons of Mary seldom bother, for they have
    inherited that good part;
But the Sons of Martha favour their Mother of the
    careful soul and the troubled heart.
And because she lost her temper once, and because
    she was rude to the Lord her Guest,
Her Sons must wait upon Mary's Sons, world with-
    out end reprieve, or rest.

It is their care in all the ages to take the buffet
    and cushion the shock.
It is their care that the gear engages; it is their
    care that the switches lock.
It is their care that the wheels run truly; it is their
    care to embark and entrain,
Tally, transport, and deliver duly the Sons of
    Mary by land and main.

They say to mountains, 'Be ye removèd.'   They
    say to the lesser floods 'Be dry.'
Under their rods are the rocks reprovèd—they are
    not afraid of that which is high.
Then do the hill-tops shake to the summit—then
    is the bed of the deep laid bare,
That the Sons of Mary may overcome it, pleasantly
    sleeping and unaware.

They finger death at their gloves' end where they
    piece and repiece the living wires.
He rears against the gates they tend: they feed
    him hungry behind their fires.
Early at dawn, ere men see clear, they stumble into
    his terrible stall,
And hale him forth like a haltered steer, and goad
    and turn him till evenfall.

To these from birth is Belief forbidden; from these
    till death is Relief afar.
They are concerned with matters hidden—under
    the earth-line their altars are:

The secret fountains to follow up, waters withdrawn
    to restore to the mouth,
And gather the floods as in a cup, and pour them
    again at a city's drouth

They do not preach that their God will rouse them
    a little before the nuts work loose.
They do not teach that His Pity allows them to
    leave their work when they damn-well choose.
As in the thronged and the lighted ways, so in the
    dark and the desert they stand,
Wary and watchful all their days that their breth-
    ren's days may be long in the land.

Raise ye the stone or cleave the wood to make a
    path more fair or flat;
Lo, it is black already with blood some Son of
    Martha spilled for that!
Not as a ladder from earth to Heaven, not as a
    witness to any creed,
But simple service simply given to his own kind in
    their common need.

And the Sons of Mary smile and are blessèd—they
    know the angels are on their side.
They know in them is the Grace confessèd, and for
    them are the Mercies multiplied.
They sit at the Feet—they hear the Word—they
    see how truly the Promise runs;
They have cast their burden upon the Lord, and—
    the Lord He lays it on Martha's Sons!

MARY'S SON

IF you stop to find out what your wages will be
  And how they will clothe and feed you,
Willie, my son, don't you go on the Sea,
  For the Sea will never need you.

If you ask for the reason of every command,
  And argue with people about you,
Willie, my son, don't you go on the Land,
  For the Land will do better without you.

If you stop to consider the work you have done
  And to boast what your labour is worth, dear,
Angels may come for you, Willie, my son,
  But you'll never be wanted on Earth, dear!

THE SONG OF THE LATHES
1918
(Being the words of the tune hummed at her lathe by
Mrs. L. Embsay, widow.)

THE fans and the beltings they roar round me.
The power is shaking the floor round me
Till the lathes pick up their duty and the midnight-
shift takes over.

It is good for me to be here!

Guns in Flanders—Flanders guns !
(I had a man that worked 'em once !)
Shells for guns in Flanders, Flanders !
Shells for guns in Flanders, Flanders !
Shells for guns in Flanders !   Feed the guns !

The cranes and the carriers they boom over me,
The bays and the galleries they loom over me,
With their quarter-mile of pillars growing little in
the distance:

It is good for me to be here!

78

The Zeppelins and Gothas they raid over us.

Our lights give warning, and fade over us.

(Seven thousand women keeping quiet in the
darkness!)

Oh, it is good for me to be here!

The roofs and the buildings they grow round me,

Eating up the fields I used to know round me;

And the shed that I began in is a sub-inspector's
office—

So long have I been here!

I've seen six hundred mornings make our lamps
grow dim,

Through the bit that isn't painted round our sky-
light rim,

And the sunshine in the window slope according to the seasons,

Twice since I've been here.

The trains on the sidings they call to us

With the hundred thousand blanks that they haul
to us;

And we send 'em what we've finished, and they
    take it where it's wanted,
        For that is why we are here!

Man's hate passes as his love will pass.
God made woman what she always was.
Them that bear the burden they will never grant
    forgiveness
        So long as they are here!

Once I was a woman, but that's by with me.
All I loved and looked for, it must die with me.
But the Lord has left me over for a servant of the
    Judgment,
        And I serve His Judgments here!

Guns in Flanders—Flanders guns !
(I had a son that worked 'em once !)
Shells for guns in Flanders, Flanders !
Shells for guns in Flanders, Flanders !
        Shells for guns in Flanders !   Feed the guns !

GETHSEMANE

The Garden called Gethsemane
  In Picardy it was,
And there the people came to see
  The English soldiers pass.
We used to pass—we used to pass
  Or halt, as it might be,
And ship our masks in case of gas
  Beyond Gethsemane.

The Garden called Gethsemane,
  It held a pretty lass,
But all the time she talked to me
  I prayed my cup might pass.
The officer sat on the chair,
  The men lay on the grass,
And all the time we halted there
  I prayed my cup might pass.

It didn't pass—it didn't pass—
It didn't pass from me.
I drank it when we met the gas
Beyond Gethsemane.

THE PRO-CONSULS

The overfaithful sword returns the user
His heart's desire at price of his heart's blood.
The clamour of the arrogant accuser
Wastes that one hour we needed to make good.
This was foretold of old at our outgoing;
This we accepted who have squandered, knowing,
The strength and glory of our reputations,
At the day's need, as it were dross, to guard
The tender and new-dedicate foundations
Against the sea we fear—not man's award.

They that dig foundations deep,
   Fit for realms to rise upon,
Little honour do they reap
   Of their generation,
Any more than mountains gain
Stature till we reach the plain.

With no veil before their face
  Such as shroud or sceptre lend—
Daily in the market-place,
  Of one height to foe and friend—
They must cheapen self to find
Ends uncheapened for mankind.

Through the night when hirelings rest,
  Sleepless they arise, alone,
The unsleeping arch to test
  And the o'er-trusted corner-stone,
'Gainst the need, they know, that lies
Hid behind the centuries.

Not by lust of praise or show
  Not by Peace herself betrayed—
Peace herself must they forego
  Till that peace be fitly made;
And in single strength uphold
  Wearier hands and hearts acold.

On the stage their act hath framed
   For thy sports, O Liberty!
Doubted are they, and defamed
   By the tongues their act set free,
While they quicken, tend and raise
Power that must their power displace

Lesser men feign greater goals,
   Failing whereof they may sit
Scholarly to judge the souls
   That go down into the pit,
And, despite its certain clay,
Heave a new world towards the day.

These at labour make no sign,
   More than planets, tides or years
Which discover God's design,
   Not our hopes and not our fears;
Nor in aught they gain or lose
Seek a triumph or excuse.

For, so the Ark be borne to Zion, who
Heeds how they perished or were paid that bore it ?
For, so the Shrine abide, what shame—what pride—
If we, the priests, were bound or crowned before it ?

THE CRAFTSMAN

ONCE, after long-drawn revel at The Mermaid,
He to the overbearing Boanerges
Jonson, uttered (If half of it were liquor,
          Blessed be the vintage!)

Saying how, at an alehouse under Cotswold,
He had made sure of his very Cleopatra,
Drunk with enormous, salvation-contemning
          Love for a tinker.

How, while he hid from Sir Thomas's keepers,
Crouched in a ditch and drenched by the midnight
Dews, he had listened to gipsy Juliet
          Rail at the dawning.

How at Bankside, a boy drowning kittens
Winced at the business; whereupon his sister
(Lady Macbeth aged seven) thrust 'em under,
          Sombrely scornful.

How on a Sabbath, hushed and compassionate—
She being known since her birth to the townsfolk—
Stratford dredged and delivered from Avon
                    Dripping Ophelia.

So, with a thin third finger marrying
Drop to wine-drop domed on the table,
Shakespeare opened his heart till sunrise
                    Entered to hear him.

London wakened and he, imperturbable,
Passed from waking to hurry after shadows . . .
Busied upon shows of no earthly importance?
                    Yes, but he knew it!

THINGS AND THE MAN

(IN MEMORIAM, JOSEPH CHAMBERLAIN)
1904

('And Joseph dreamed a dream, and he told it his brethren:
and they hated him yet the more.'—*Genesis* xxxvii. 5.)

OH ye who hold the written clue
  To all save all unwritten things,
And, half a league behind, pursue
    The accomplished Fact with flouts and flings,
    Look!   To your knee your baby brings
      The oldest tale since Earth began—
    The answer to your worryings:
      'Once on a time there was a Man.'

He, single-handed, met and slew
  Magicians, Armies, Ogres, Kings.
He lonely 'mid his doubting crew—
    'In all the loneliness of wings'—

He fed the flame, he filled the springs,
 He locked the ranks, he launched the van
Straight at the grinning Teeth of Things.
 '*Once on a time there was a Man.*'

The peace of shocked Foundations flew
 Before his ribald questionings.
He broke the Oracles in two,
 And bared the paltry wires and strings.
 He headed desert wanderings;
  He led his soul, his cause, his clan
 A little from the ruck of Things.
  '*Once on a time there was a Man.*'

Thrones, Powers, Dominions block the view
 With episodes and underlings—
The meek historian deems them true
 Nor heeds the song that Clio sings—
 The simple central truth that stings
  The mob to boo, the priest to ban;
 Things never yet created things—
  '*Once on a time there was a Man.*'

A bolt is fallen from the blue.

   A wakened realm full circle swings

Where Dothan's dreamer dreams anew

   Of vast and farborne harvestings;

   And unto him an Empire clings

     That grips the purpose of his plan.

     My Lords, how think you of these things?

      Once—in our time—is there a Man ?

THE BENEFACTORS

Ah! What avails the classic bent
And what the cultured word,
Against the undoctored incident
That actually occurred?

And what is Art whereto we press
Through paint and prose and rhyme—
When Nature in her nakedness
Defeats us every time?

It is not learning, grace nor gear,
Nor easy meat and drink,
But bitter pinch of pain and fear
That makes creation think.

When in this world's unpleasing youth
  Our god-like race began,
The longest arm, the sharpest tooth,
  Gave man control of man;

Till, bruised and bitten to the bone
  And taught by pain and fear,
He learned to deal the far-off stone,
  And poke the long, safe spear.

So tooth and nail were obsolete
  As means against a foe,
Till, bored by uniform defeat,
  Some genius built the bow.

Then stone and javelin proved as vain
  As old-time tooth and nail;
Ere, spurred anew by fear and pain,
  Man fashioned coats of mail.

Then was there safety for the rich
   And danger for the poor,
Till someone mixed a powder which
   Redressed the scale once more.

Helmet and armour disappeared
   With sword and bow and pike,
And, when the smoke of battle cleared,
   All men were armed alike. . . .

And when ten million such were slain
   To please one crazy king,
Man, schooled in bulk by fear and pain,
   Grew weary of the thing;

And, at the very hour designed,
   To enslave him past recall,
His tooth-stone-arrow-gun-shy mind
   Turned and abolished all.

     .   .   .   .

All Power, each Tyrant, every Mob
Whose head has grown too large,
Ends by destroying its own job
And earns its own discharge.

And Man, whose mere necessities
Move all things from his path,
Trembles meanwhile at their decrees,
And deprecates their wrath!

THE DEAD KING

(EDWARD VII.)

1910

*Who in the Realm to-day lays down dear life for the
sake of a land more dear ?
And, unconcerned for his own estate, toils till the last
grudged sands have run ?
    Let him approach.   It is proven here
Our King asks nothing of any man more than Our
King himself has done.*

For to him above all was Life good, above all he
   commanded
      Her abundance full-handed.

The peculiar treasure of Kings was his for the
taking:

All that men come to in dreams he inherited
waking:—

His marvel of world-gathered armies—one heart
and all races;

His seas 'neath his keels when his war-castles
foamed to their places;

The thundering foreshores that answered his
heralded landing;

The huge lighted cities adoring, the assemblies
upstanding;

The Councils of Kings called in haste to learn how
he was minded—

The Kingdoms, the Powers, and the Glories he
dealt with unblinded.

To him came all captains of men, all achievers of
glory,

Hot from the press of their battles they told him
their story.

They revealed him their life in an hour and, saluting,
    departed,
Joyful to labour afresh—he had made them new-
    hearted.
And, since he weighed men from his youth, and no
    lie long deceived him,
He spoke and exacted the truth, and the basest
    believed him.

And God poured him an exquisite wine, that was
    daily renewed to him,
In the clear-welling love of his peoples that daily
    accrued to him.
Honour and service we gave him, rejoicingly
    fearless;
Faith absolute, trust beyond speech and a friendship
    as peerless.
And since he was Master and Servant in all that we
    asked him,
We leaned hard on his wisdom in all things, know-
    ing not how we tasked him.

For on him each new day laid command, every
    tyrannous hour,

To confront, or confirm, or make smooth some dread
    issue of power;

To deliver true judgment aright at the instant,
    unaided,

In the strict, level, ultimate phrase that allowed or
    dissuaded;

To foresee, to allay, to avert from us perils un-
    numbered,

To stand guard on our gates when he guessed that
    the watchmen had slumbered;

To win time, to turn hate, to woo folly to service
    and, mightily schooling

His strength to the use of his Nations, to rule as
    not ruling.

These were the works of our King; Earth's peace
    was the proof of them.

God gave him great works to fulfil, and to us the
    behoof of them.

We accepted his toil as our right—none spared,
    none excused him.
When he was bowed by his burden his rest was
    refused him.
We troubled his age with our weakness—the blacker
    our shame to us!
Hearing his People had need of him, straightway
    he came to us.

As he received so he gave—nothing grudged,
    naught denying,
Not even the last gasp of his breath when he strove
    for us, dying.
For our sakes, without question, he put from him
    all that he cherished.
Simply as any that serve him he served and he
    perished.
All that Kings covet was his, and he flung it aside
    for us.
Simply as any that die in his service he died for us.

Who in the Realm to-day has choice of the easy road or
  the hard to tread ?
And, much concerned for his own estate, would sell
  his soul to remain in the sun ?
    Let him depart nor look on Our dead.
Our King asks nothing of any man more than Our
  King himself has done.

A DEATH-BED

'THIS is the State above the Law.
  The State exists for the State alone.'
[*This is a gland at the back of the jaw,
  And an answering lump by the collar-bone.*]

Some die shouting in gas or fire;
  Some die silent, by shell and shot.
Some die desperate, caught on the wire;
  Some die suddenly.   This will not.

'Regis suprema Voluntas lex'
  [*It will follow the regular course of—throats.*]
Some die pinned by the broken decks,
  Some die sobbing between the boats.

Some die eloquent, pressed to death
  By the sliding trench as their friends can hear.
Some die wholly in half a breath.
  Some—give trouble for half a year.

'There is neither Evil nor Good in life
   Except as the needs of the State ordain.'
[*Since it is rather too late for the knife,*
   All we can do is to mask the pain.]

Some die saintly in faith and hope—
   One died thus in a prison-yard—
Some die broken by rape or the rope;
   Some die easily.   This dies hard.

'I will dash to pieces who bar my way.
   Woe to the traitor!   Woe to the weak!'
[*Let him write what he wishes to say.*
   It tires him out if he tries to speak.]

Some die quietly.   Some abound
   In loud self-pity.   Others spread
Bad morale through the cots around . . .
   This is a type that is better dead.

'The war was forced on me by my foes.
   All that I sought was the right to live.'
Don't be afraid of a triple dose;
   The pain will neutralize half we give.

Here are the needles.   See that he dies
   While the effects of the drug endure.   .   .   .
What is the question he asks with his eyes ?—
   Yes, All-Highest, to God, be sure.]

GEHAZI

'WHENCE comest thou, Gehazi,
    So reverend to behold,
In scarlet and in ermines
    And chain of England's gold?'
'From following after Naaman
    To tell him all is well,
Whereby, my zeal hath made me
    A Judge in Israel.'

Well done, well done, Gehazi,
    Stretch forth thy ready hand,
Thou barely 'scaped from judgment,
    Take oath to judge the land,
Unswayed by gift of money
    Or privy bribe, more base,
Of knowledge which is profit
    In any market-place.

Search out and probe, Gehazi,
　As thou of all canst try,
The truthful, well-weighed answer
　That tells the blacker lie—
The loud, uneasy virtue
　The anger feigned at will,
To overbear a witness
　And make the Court keep still.

Take order now, Gehazi,
　That no man talk aside
In secret with his judges
　The while his case is tried.
Lest he should show them—reason
　To keep a matter hid,
And subtly lead the questions
　Away from what he did.

Thou mirror of uprightness,
　What ails thee at thy vows?
What means the risen whiteness
　Of the skin between thy brows?

The boils that shine and burrow,
  The sores that slough and bleed—
The leprosy of Naaman
  On thee and all thy seed?
   Stand up, stand up, Gehazi,
    Draw close thy robe and go,
   Gehazi, Judge in Israel,
    A leper white as snow!

THE VIRGINITY

TRY as he will, no man breaks wholly loose
From his first love, no matter who she be.
Oh, was there ever sailor free to choose,
That didn't settle somewhere near the sea?

Myself, it don't excite me nor amuse
To watch a pack o' shipping on the sea,
But I can understand my neighbour's views
From certain things which have occurred to me.

Men must keep touch with things they used to use
To earn their living, even when they are free;
And so come back upon the least excuse—
Same as the sailor settled near the sea.

He knows he's never going on no cruise—
He knows he's done and finished with the sea;
And yet he likes to feel she's there to use—
If he should ask her—as she used to be.

Even though she cost him all he had to lose,
Even though she made him sick to hear or see,
Still, what she left of him will mostly choose
Her skirts to sit by. How comes such to be?

Parsons in pulpits, tax-payers in pews,
Kings on your thrones, you know as well as me,
We've only one virginity to lose,
And where we lost it there our hearts will be!

A PILGRIM'S WAY

I do not look for holy saints to guide me on my
way,
Or male and female devilkins to lead my feet
astray.
If these are added, I rejoice—if not, I shall not
mind,
So long as I have leave and choice to meet my
fellow-kind.
For as we come and as we go (and deadly soon
go we!)
The people, Lord, Thy people, are good enough
for me!

Thus I will honour pious men whose virtue shines
so bright
(Though none are more amazed than I when I by
chance do right),

And I will pity foolish men for woe their sins have
    bred
(Though ninety-nine per cent. of mine I brought on
    my own head).
    And, Amorite or Eremite, or General Averagee,
    The people, Lord, Thy people, are good enough
        for me!

And when they bore me overmuch, I will not shake
    mine ears,
Recalling many thousand such whom I have bored
    to tears.
And when they labour to impress, I will not doubt
    nor scoff;
Since I myself have done no less and—sometimes
    pulled it off.
    Yea, as we are and we are not, and we pretend
      to be,
    The people, Lord, Thy people, are good enough
        for me!

And when they work me random wrong, as often-
    times hath been,
I will not cherish hate too long (my hands are none
    too clean).
And when they do me random good I will not feign
    ⸗ surprise,
No more than those whom I have cheered with
    wayside charities.
    But, as we give and as we take—whate'er our
        takings be—
    The people, Lord, Thy people, are good enough
        for me!

But when I meet with frantic folk who sinfully de-
    clare
There is no pardon for their sin, the same I will
    not spare
Till I have proved that Heaven and Hell which in
    our hearts we have
Show nothing irredeemable on either side the grave.

For as we live and as we die—if utter Death there
be—
The people, Lord, Thy people, are good enough
for me!

Deliver me from every pride—the Middle, High,
and Low—
That bars me from a brother's side, whatever state
he show.
And purge me from all heresies of thought and
speech and pen
That bid me judge him otherwise than I am judged.
  Amen !
  That I may sing of Crowd or King or road-borne
  company,
  That I may labour in my day, vocation and
  degree,
  To prove the same in deed and name, and hold
  unshakenly
  (Where'er I go, whate'er I know, whoe'er my
  neighbour be)

This single faith in Life and Death and all
    Eternity:
'The people, Lord, Thy people, are good enough
    for me!'

THE OLDEST SONG

(For before Eve was Lilith.—*Old Tale.*)

THESE were never your true love's eyes.
　Why do you feign that you love them?
You that broke from their constancies,
　And the wide calm brows above them!

This was never your true love's speech.
　Why do you thrill when you hear it?
You that have ridden out of its reach
　The width of the world or near it!

This was never your true love's hair,—
　You that chafed when it bound you
Screened from knowledge or shame or care,
　In the night that it made around you!

 '*All these things I know, I know.*
   And that's why my heart is breaking !'
Then what do you gain by pretending so?
  '*The joy of an old wound waking.*'

NATURAL THEOLOGY

PRIMITIVE

I ATE my fill of a whale that died
    And stranded after a month at sea. . . .
There is a pain in my inside.
    Why have the Gods afflicted me?
Ow! I am purged till I am a wraith!
    Wow! I am sick till I cannot see!
What is the sense of Religion and Faith?
    Look how the Gods have afflicted me!

PAGAN

How can the skin of rat or mouse hold
    Anything more than a harmless flea? . . .
The burning plague has taken my household.
    Why have my Gods afflicted me?

All my kith and kin are deceased,
    Though they were as good as good could be.
I will out and batter the family priest,
    Because my Gods have afflicted me.

MEDIÆVAL

My privy and well drain into each other
    After the custom of Christendie. . . .
Fevers and fluxes are wasting my mother.
    Why has the Lord afflicted me?
The Saints are helpless for all I offer—
    So are the clergy I used to fee.
Henceforward I keep my cash in my coffer,
    Because the Lord has afflicted me.

MATERIAL

I run eight hundred hens to the acre.
    They die by dozens mysteriously. . . .
I am more than doubtful concerning my Maker.
    Why has the Lord afflicted me?

What a return for all my endeavour—
   Not to mention the L. S. D.!
I am an atheist now and for ever,
   Because this God has afflicted me!

PROGRESSIVE

Money spent on an Army or Fleet
   Is homicidal lunacy. . . .
My son has been killed in the Mons retreat.
   Why is the Lord afflicting me?
Why are murder, pillage and arson
   And rape allowed by the Deity?
I will write to the *Times*, deriding our parson,
   Because my God has afflicted me.

CHORUS

We had a kettle: we let it leak:
   Our not repairing it made it worse.
We haven't had any tea for a week. . . .
   The bottom is out of the Universe!

CONCLUSION

This was none of the good Lord's pleasure,
　For the Spirit He breathed in Man is free;
But what comes after is measure for measure,
　And not a God that afflicteth thee.
As was the sowing so the reaping
　Is now and evermore shall be.
Thou art delivered to thy own keeping.
　Only Thyself hath afflicted thee!

A SONG AT COCK-CROW

'Ille autem iterum negavit.'

THE first time that Peter deniéd his Lord
He shrank from the cudgel, the scourge and the
    cord,
But followed far off to see what they would do,
Till the cock crew—till the cock crew—
After Gethsemane, till the cock crew!

The first time that Peter deniéd his Lord
'Twas only a maid in the palace who heard,
As he sat by the fire and warmed himself through.
Then the cock crew!   Then the cock crew!
('Thou also art one of them.')   Then the cock crew!

The first time that Peter deniéd his Lord
He had neither the Throne, nor the Keys nor the
    Sword—

A poor silly fisherman, what could he do
When the cock crew—when the cock crew—
But weep for his wickedness when the cock crew?

. . . .

The next time that Peter deniéd his Lord
He was Fisher of Men, as foretold by the Word,
With the Crown on his brow and the Cross on his
    shoe,
When the cock crew—when the cock crew—
In Flanders and Picardy when the cock crew.

The next time that Peter deniéd his Lord
'Twas Mary the Mother in Heaven Who heard,
And She grieved for the maidens and wives that
    they slew
When the cock crew—when the cock crew—
At Tirmonde and Aerschott when the cock crew.

The next time that Peter deniéd his Lord
The Babe in the Manger awakened and stirred,

And He stretched out His arms for the playmates
    He knew—
When the cock crew—when the cock crew—
But the waters had covered them when the cock crew.

The next time that Peter deniéd his Lord
'Twas Earth in her agony waited his word,
But he sat by the fire and naught would he do,
Though the cock crew—though the cock crew—
Over all Christendom, though the cock crew.

The last time that Peter deniéd his Lord,
The Father took from him the Keys and the Sword,
And the Mother and Babe brake his Kingdom in
    two,
When the cock crew—when the cock crew—
(Because of his wickedness) when the cock crew!

THE FEMALE OF THE SPECIES

1911

WHEN the Himalayan peasant meets the he-bear in
    his pride,
He shouts to scare the monster, who will often turn
    aside.
But the she-bear thus accosted rends the peasant
    tooth and nail.
For the female of the species is more deadly than
    the male.

When Nag the basking cobra hears the careless
    foot of man,
He will sometimes wriggle sideways and avoid it as
    he can.

But his mate makes no such motion where she
  camps beside the trail.
For the female of the species is more deadly than
  the male.

When the early Jesuit fathers preached to Hurons
  and Choctaws,
They prayed to be delivered from the vengeance of
  the squaws.
'Twas the women, not the warriors, turned those
  stark enthusiasts pale.
For the female of the species is more deadly than
  the male.

Man's timid heart is bursting with the things he
  must not say,
For the Woman that God gave him isn't his to
  give away;

But when hunter meets with husband, each confirms
    the other's tale—
The female of the species is more deadly than the
    male.

Man, a bear in most relations—worm and savage
    otherwise,—
Man propounds negotiations, Man accepts the
    compromise.
Very rarely will he squarely push the logic of
    a fact
To its ultimate conclusion in unmitigated act.

Fear, or foolishness, impels him, ere he lay the
    wicked low,
To concede some form of trial even to his fiercest
    foe.

Mirth obscene diverts his anger! Doubt and Pity
    oft perplex
Him in dealing with an issue—to the scandal of
    The Sex!

But the Woman that God gave him, every fibre of
    her frame
Proves her launched for one sole issue, armed and
    engined for the same;
And to serve that single issue, lest the generations
    fail,
The female of the species must be deadlier than
    the male.

She who faces Death by torture for each life
    beneath her breast
May not deal in doubt or pity—must not swerve
    for fact or jest.

These be purely male diversions—not in these her
honour dwells.
She the Other Law we live by, is that Law and
nothing else.

She can bring no more to living than the powers
that make her great
As the Mother of the Infant and the Mistress of
the Mate!
And when Babe and Man are lacking and she
strides unclaimed to claim
Her right as femme (and baron), her equipment is
the same.

She is wedded to convictions—in default of grosser
ties;
Her contentions are her children, Heaven help him
who denies!—

He will meet no suave discussion, but the instant,
  white-hot, wild,
Wakened female of the species warring as for
  spouse and child.

Unprovoked and awful charges—even so the she-
  bear fights,
Speech that drips, corrodes, and poisons—even so
  the cobra bites,
Scientific vivisection of one nerve till it is
  raw
And the victim writhes in anguish—like the Jesuit
  with the squaw!

So it comes that Man the coward, when he gathers
  to confer
With his fellow-braves in council, dare not leave
  a place for her

Where, at war with Life and Conscience, he uplifts
    his erring hands
To some God of Abstract Justice—which no woman
    understands.

And Man knows it! Knows, moreover, that the
    Woman that God gave him
Must command but may not govern—shall enthral
    but not enslave him.
And *She* knows, because She warns him, and Her
    instincts never fail,
That the Female of Her Species is more deadly
    than the Male.

EPITAPHS

'Equality of Sacrifice'

A. 'I was a "have."' *B.* 'I was a "have-not."'
(*Together*). 'What hast thou given which I gave
    not?'

A Servant

We were together since the War began.
He was my servant—and the better man.

A Son

My son was killed while laughing at some jest. I
    would I knew
What it was, and it might serve me in a time when
    jests are few.

An Only Son

I have slain none except my Mother. She
(Blessing her slayer) died of grief for me.

Ex-Clerk

Pity not!   The Army gave
Freedom to a timid slave:
In which Freedom did he find
Strength of body, will, and mind:
By which strength he came to prove
Mirth, Companionship, and Love:
For which Love to Death he went:
In which Death he lies content.

The Wonder

Body and Spirit I surrendered whole
To harsh Instructors—and received a soul . . .
If mortal man could change me through and
    through
From all I was—what may The God not do?

HINDU SEPOY IN FRANCE

This man in his own country prayed we know not
    to what Powers.
We pray Them to reward him for his bravery in
    ours.

THE COWARD

I could not look on Death, which being known,
Men led me to him, blindfold and alone.

SHOCK

My name, my speech, my self I had forgot.
My wife and children came—I knew them not.
I died.   My Mother followed.   At her call
And on her bosom I remembered all.

A Grave near Cairo

Gods of the Nile, should this stout fellow here
Get out—get out! He knows not shame nor fear.

Pelicans in the Wilderness

(A grave near Halfa)

The blown sand heaps on me, that none may learn
  Where I am laid for whom my children grieve. . .
O wings that beat at dawning, ye return
  Out of the desert to your young at eve!

The Favour

Death favoured me from the first, well knowing I
    could not endure
  To wait on him day by day. He quitted my
    betters and came

Whistling over the fields, and, when he had made
    all sure,
  'Thy line is at end,' he said, 'but at least I have
    saved its name."

THE BEGINNER

On the first hour of my first day
    In the front trench I fell.
(Children in boxes at a play
    Stand up to watch it well.)

R. A. F. (AGED EIGHTEEN)

Laughing through clouds, his milk-teeth still un-
    shed,
Cities and men he smote from overhead.
His deaths delivered, he returned to play
Childlike, with childish things now put away.

The Refined Man

I was of delicate mind.   I went aside for my needs,
   Disdaining the common office.   I was seen from
      afar and killed.   .   .   .
How is this matter for mirth?   Let each man be
   judged by his deeds.
   I have paid my price to live with myself on the terms
      that I willed.

Native Water-Carrier (M. E. F.)

Prometheus brought down fire to men.
   This brought up water.
The Gods are jealous—now, as then,
   They gave no quarter.

Bombed in London

On land and sea I strove with anxious care
To escape conscription.   It was in the air!

THE SLEEPY SENTINEL

Faithless the watch that I kept: now I have none
    to keep.
I was slain because I slept: now I am slain I sleep.
Let no man reproach me again, whatever watch is
    unkept—
I sleep because I am slain.　They slew me because
    I slept.

BATTERIES OUT OF AMMUNITION

If any mourn us in the workshop, say
We died because the shift kept holiday.

COMMON FORM

If any question why we died,
Tell them, because our fathers lied.

A DEAD STATESMAN

I could not dig: I dared not rob:
Therefore I lied to please the mob.

Now all my lies are proved untrue,
And I must face the men I slew.
What tale shall save me here among
Mine angry and defrauded young?

THE REBEL

If I had clamoured at Thy Gate
    For gift of Life on Earth,
And, thrusting through the souls that wait,
    Flung headlong into birth—
Even then, even then, for gin and snare
    About my pathway spread,
Lord, I had mocked Thy thoughtful care
    Before I joined the Dead!
But now? . . . I was beneath Thy Hand
    Ere yet the Planets came.
And now—though Planets pass, I stand
    The witness to Thy Shame.

The Obedient

Daily, though no ears attended,
　Did my prayers arise.
Daily, though no fire descended
　Did I sacrifice. . . .
Though my darkness did not lift,
　Though I faced no lighter odds,
Though the Gods bestowed no gift,
　　　　　None the less,
　None the less, I served the Gods!

A Drifter off Tarentum

He from the wind-bitten north with ship and
　companions descended,
　Searching for eggs of death spawned by invisible
　hulls.
Many he found and drew forth. Of a sudden the
　fishery ended
　In flame and a clamorous breath not new to the
　eye-pecking gulls.

DESTROYERS IN COLLISION

For Fog and Fate no charm is found
    To lighten or amend.
I, hurrying to my bride, was drowned—
    Cut down by my best friend.

CONVOY ESCORT

I was a shepherd to fools
    Causelessly bold or afraid.
They would not abide by my rules.
    Yet they escaped. For I stayed.

UNKNOWN FEMALE CORPSE

Headless, lacking foot and hand,
Horrible I come to land.
I beseech all women's sons
Know I was a mother once.

RAPED AND REVENGED

One used and butchered me: another spied
Me broken—for which thing a hundred died.
So it was learned among the heathen hosts
How much a freeborn woman's favour costs.

SALONIKAN GRAVE

I have watched a thousand days
Push out and crawl into night
Slowly as tortoises.
Now I, too, follow these.
It is fever, and not fight—
Time, not battle—that slays.

THE BRIDEGROOM

Call me not false, beloved,
    If, from thy scarce-known breast
So little time removed,
    In other arms I rest.

For this more ancient bride
   Whom coldly I embrace
Was constant at my side
   Before I saw thy face.

Our marriage, often set—
   By miracle delayed—
At last is consummate,
   And cannot be unmade.

Live, then, whom Life shall cure,
   Almost, of Memory,
And leave us to endure
   Its immortality.

V. A. D. (Mediterranean)

Ah, would swift ships had never been, for then we
   ne'er had found,
These harsh Ægean rocks between, this little virgin
   drowned,

Whom neither spouse nor child shall mourn, but
    men she nursed through pain
And—certain keels for whose return the heathen
    look in vain.

'THE CITY OF BRASS'

1909

('Here was a people whom after their works thou shalt see wept over for their lost dominion: and in this palace is the last information respecting lords collected in the dust.'—*The Arabian Nights.*)

*In a land that the sand overlays—the ways to her gates
    are untrod—*

*A multitude ended their days whose fates were made
    splendid by God,*

*Till they grew drunk and were smitten with madness
    and went to their fall,*

*And of these is a story written: but Allah alone
    knoweth all !*

When the wine stirred in their heart their bosoms
    dilated,

They rose to suppose themselves kings over all
    things created—

To decree a new earth at a birth without labour or
  sorrow—
To declare: 'We prepare it to-day and inherit
  to-morrow.'
They chose themselves prophets and priests of
  minute understanding,
Men swift to see done, and outrun, their extremest
  commanding—
Of the tribe which describe with a jibe the per-
  versions of Justice—
Panders avowed to the crowd whatsoever its lust is.

Swiftly these pulled down the walls that their
  fathers had made them—
The impregnable ramparts of old, they razed and
  relaid them
As playgrounds of pleasure and leisure with limit-
  less entries,
And havens of rest for the wastrels where once
  walked the sentries;

And because there was need of more pay for the
    shouters and marchers,

They disbanded in face of their foemen their bow-
    men and archers.

They replied to their well-wishers' fears—to their
    enemies' laughter,

Saying: 'Peace! We have fashioned a God Which
    shall save us hereafter.

We ascribe all dominion to man in his factions
    conferring,

And have given to numbers the Name of the
    Wisdom unerring.'

They said: 'Who has hate in his soul? Who has
    envied his neighbour?

Let him arise and control both that man and his
    labour.'

They said: 'Who is eaten by sloth? Whose un-
    thrift has destroyed him?

He shall levy a tribute from all because none have
    employed him.'

They said: 'Who hath toiled? Who hath striven,
    and gathered possession?

Let him be spoiled. He hath given full proof of
    transgression.'

They said: 'Who is irked by the Law? *Though
    we may not remove it,*

*If he lend us his aid in this raid, we will set him above
    it !'*

So the robber did judgment again upon such as
    displeased him,

The slayer, too, boasted his slain, and the judges
    released him.

As for their kinsmen far off, on the skirts of the
    nation,

They harried all earth to make sure none escaped
    reprobation,

They awakened unrest for a jest in their newly-
    won borders,

And jeered at the blood of their brethren betrayed
    by their orders.

They instructed the ruled to rebel, their rulers to
    aid them;

And, since such as obeyed them not fell, their
    Viceroys obeyed them.

When the riotous set them at naught they said:
    'Praise the upheaval!

For the show and the word and the thought of
    Dominion is evil!'

They unwound and flung from them with rage, as a
    rag that defiled them

The imperial gains of the age which their fore-
    fathers piled them.

They ran panting in haste to lay waste and em-
    bitter for ever

The wellsprings of Wisdom and Strength which are
    Faith and Endeavour.

They nosed out and digged up and dragged forth
    and exposed to derision

All doctrine of purpose and worth and restraint and
    prevision:

And it ceased, and God granted them all things
    for which they had striven,
And the heart of a beast in the place of a man's
    heart was given. . . .
  .   .   .   .

When they were fullest of wine and most flagrant
    in error,
Out of the sea rose a sign—out of Heaven a
    terror.
Then they saw, then they heard, then they knew—
    for none troubled to hide it,
An host had prepared their destruction, but still
    they denied it.
They denied what they dared not abide if it came
    to the trial,
But the Sword that was forged while they lied did
    not heed their denial.
It drove home, and no time was allowed to the
    crowd that was driven.
The preposterous-minded were cowed—they thought
    time would be given.

There was no need of a steed nor a lance to pursue
    them;

It was decreed their own deed, and not chance,
    should undo them.

The tares they had laughingly sown were ripe to
    the reaping,

The trust they had leagued to disown was removed
    from their keeping.

The eaters of other men's bread, the exempted
    from hardship,

The excusers of impotence fled, abdicating their
    wardship.

For the hate they had taught through the State
    brought the State no defender,

And it passed from the roll of the Nations in head-
    long surrender.

JUSTICE

October 1918

Across a world where all men grieve
  And grieving strive the more,
The great days range like tides and leave
  Our dead on every shore.
Heavy the load we undergo,
  And our own hands prepare,
If we have parley with the foe,
  The load our sons must bear.

Before we loose the word
  That bids new worlds to birth,
Needs must we loosen first the sword
  Of Justice upon earth;

Or else all else is vain
　　Since life on earth began,
And the spent world sinks back again
　　Hopeless of God and Man.

A people and their King
　　Through ancient sin grown strong,
Because they feared no reckoning
　　Would set no bound to wrong;
But now their hour is past,
　　And we who bore it find
Evil Incarnate held at last
　　To answer to mankind.

For agony and spoil
　　Of nations beat to dust,
For poisoned air and tortured soil
　　And cold, commanded lust,
And every secret woe
　　The shuddering waters saw—
Willed and fulfilled by high and low—
　　Let them relearn the Law.

That when the dooms are read,
    Not high nor low shall say:—
'My haughty or my humble head
    Has saved me in this day.'
That, till the end of time,
    Their remnant shall recall
Their fathers' old, confederate crime
    Availed them not at all.

That neither schools nor priests,
    Nor Kings may build again
A people with the heart of beasts
    Made wise concerning men.
Whereby our dead shall sleep
    In honour, unbetrayed,
And we in faith and honour keep
That peace for which they paid.

THE END

THE COUNTRY LIFE PRESS
GARDEN CITY, N. Y.